rust

A PRACTICAL GUIDE TO

THE PUPIL PREMIUM

MARC ROWLAND

A JOHN CATT PUBLICATION

First published 2014
by John Catt Educational Ltd,
12 Deben Mill Business Centre, Old Maltings Approach,
Melton, Woodbridge IP12 1BL
Tel: +44 (0) 1394 389850
Fax: +44 (0) 1394 386893
Email: enquiries@johncatt.com
Website: www.johncatt.com

ISBN: 978 1 909717 20 6

Set and designed by Theoria Design Ltd
www.theoriadesign.com

Printed and bound in Great Britain
by Cambrian Printers, Aberystwyth

Contents

Foreword

by Rt Hon David Laws MP, Minister of State for Schools

I have always believed that the Pupil Premium is capable of achieving great things in our schools and in our society. The major challenge facing us has been to ensure that it makes a real difference to the disadvantaged pupils at whom it is aimed. It is critical that schools can and do use this additional funding effectively.

As a coalition government, we resisted the temptation to micromanage how schools spend the Pupil Premium and instead have given schools genuine freedom to use their own judgement on which educational interventions to fund. Alongside this freedom, we have now put in place a rigorous accountability framework that holds schools clearly to account for the progress and attainment of their disadvantaged pupils.

Since September 2013, school inspections have been more focussed on the attainment and progress of disadvantaged pupils, and how schools are closing the gap between them and their peers. Schools will not normally be judged 'Outstanding' if disadvantaged pupils are not making at least good progress. The school performance tables include details of the attainment of disadvantaged pupils and the in-school gap between them and their peers, reported for that year and as an average over the last three years.

The Pupil Premium is a significant investment in schools – £6.25 billion overall between 2011 and 2015 – so it is right that clear and fair accountability measures are in place around it.

It is still early in the implementation of the Pupil Premium to consider the full impact of this additional funding on disadvantaged pupils but a positive picture is beginning to emerge. We know that good practice in use of the Pupil Premium is already widespread and can be found in an increasing number of schools.

Ofsted tells us that more schools are getting it right when it comes to the effective use of their Pupil Premium funding. Its 2013 report, *'The Pupil Premium: how schools are spending the funding successfully to maximise achievement'*, identified the shared characteristics of schools who spent their Pupil Premium funding successfully. These included drawing on research evidence, such as the Sutton Trust toolkit, and evidence from their own and others' experience to allocate the funding to the activities that were most likely to have an impact on improving achievement; and a thorough analysis of which pupils were underachieving, particularly in English and mathematics, and why.

A new report, *'The Pupil Premium – an update'* which was published on 16 July noted that schools are now spending their Pupil Premium more effectively than at any time since its introduction in April 2011. The report also shows that gaps in attainment are closing more quickly in schools judged as "Good" or better.

On the 25 June 2014, I had the pleasure of attending the second annual Pupil Premium Awards ceremony. All of the schools involved have done extraordinary work to raise the aspiration and achievement of their disadvantaged pupils through sustainable and evidence-based school improvement. We want to see this exemplary practice spread throughout the system. We also want to continue to celebrate and reward exceptional schools and have announced enhanced awards in 2015 and 2016.

The use of research evidence to inform decision making is a key characteristic of all schools that make effective use of their Pupil Premium funding. I am pleased that this guide acknowledges the invaluable work the Education Endowment Foundation (EEF) is doing in this area. We strongly encourage schools to use the EEF teaching and learning toolkit when deciding how to invest their Pupil Premium funding. The toolkit sets out those interventions which have the best evidence for impact on pupil attainment and cost effectiveness. It is regularly refreshed to reflect the latest evidence from robust research studies, including the EEF's own projects.

I am passionate about reducing the inequalities in our education system. The evidence from the Pupil Premium Award winners is clear – the Pupil Premium can make a real difference to achievement and attainment of disadvantaged pupils. Our challenge now is to make sure that the good practice embodied by these schools and that which is set out in this publication, rooted in the National Education Trust's findings, is spread and embedded throughout the whole system.

David Laws
September 2014

Introduction

Over the past two years, I have been fortunate to visit more than 100 schools across the country to discuss and review how they are using the Pupil Premium grant to improve outcomes for disadvantaged learners. In this Practical Guide I have tried to capture the essentials for success in narrowing the gap, and to share some examples of innovation and excellence which will be useful to schools.

At the heart of every successful school, strong leadership of the Pupil Premium underpins that success. The ambitions for the pupils are driven by values, by ambition for the school community. Meeting accountability targets and Ofsted grades are a by-product, not the end goal. Clarity of purpose and clarity of aims are fundamental. Great schools are a cradle for resilient, effective and confident learners regardless of their socio-economic background.

In 2011, the Pupil Premium was introduced by the coalition government. Its aims were twofold: to improve outcomes for disadvantaged learners; and to narrow the attainment gap between them and their more affluent peers.

The Pupil Premium has become a high profile and popular policy helping schools challenge the underperformance of disadvantaged learners. In the 2014-15 financial year, the premium is £1300 per primary-age pupil, and £935 per secondary-age pupil. These represent considerable sums of money.

Whatever your view on the policy, it has shone a harsh light on the underperformance of the broad range of pupils, defined as 'disadvantaged' by the DfE, including those who live chaotic and challenging lives. In our current education system, only a third of disadvantaged students leave school with what might be considered a basic entitlement, one which will give them real choices about their future. In 2013, only 38% of disadvantaged learners got at least five A*-C including English and maths, compared to 65% of their peers

Furthermore, throughout the country there are significant variations in how disadvantaged pupils perform, and in a number of local authorities the educational outlook for disadvantaged children has been extremely poor. The 2013 KS2 results illustrate this well.

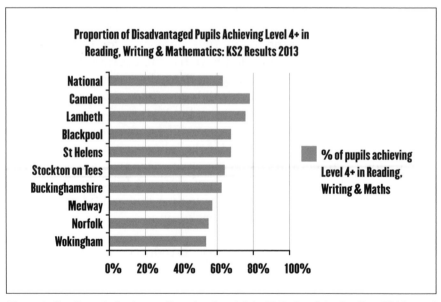

Figure 1: Key Stage 2 Attainment Data in selected LAs 2013: Level 4+ Reading, Writing and Mathematics (Disadvantaged).

It is worth highlighting how high attainers eligible for Pupil Premium perform. In 2012, an average of 2% of disadvantaged pupils achieved an A or A* in English and maths at GCSE. At the same time, an average of 10% of 'other' children achieved the same grade. In some LAs this figure is over 25% for 'other' pupils, and less than 1% for disadvantaged learners.

If ever there was a set of statistics that set out the moral imperative for a national policy, it is that one.

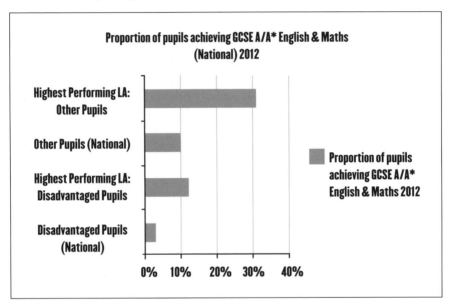

Figure 2: Key Stage 4 Results 2012 (from Department of Education).

The primary tool for narrowing gaps is high quality teaching and learning. Poor teaching has a disproportionate effect on disadvantaged learners. The good news is that high quality teaching has a disproportionately positive impact on disadvantaged learners too!

Consistently, the National Education Trust view mirrors that of Andreas Schleicher of the OECD: 'Our data shows it doesn't matter if you go to a school in Britain, Finland or Japan, students from a privileged background tend to do well everywhere. What really distinguishes education systems is their capacity to deploy resources where they can make the most difference. Your effect as a teacher is a lot bigger for a student who doesn't have a privileged background than for a student who has lots of educational resources.'

Put more simply, one of the best measures of an advanced education system is how it treats pupils who are on the margins. The Pupil Premium need not be about complete equality of outcome, but it can give every student in the schooling system the same opportunities to succeed. High quality teaching and learning is fundamental to narrowing the gap.

A note for readers: this Guide refers to National Curriculum Levels which have been at the heart of measuring pupils' progress and attainment in recent years, and these are useful to tell the Pupil Premium story to date. Schools are now properly exploring different ways of recording pupils' progress – 'life beyond levels' – and we at the National Education Trust are working to share best emerging practice in this new era: please visit www.nationaleducationtrust.net

Marc Rowland
Deputy Director, National Education Trust
September 2014

Part One

1. Policy Challenges, Practical Challenges

'Statistics should be used to shine a light, not for a crutch'

Narrowing the attainment gap within the context of an overall raising of standards is *the* great challenge for our education system. One of the easiest ways to narrow the gap is to have low attainment overall. Clearly though, it is much better for a primary school to have most pupils at L4b+ with a gap, instead of 60% L4b+ for all. Thus, closing the gap through a drop in attainment for non-disadvantaged pupils is not something to celebrate – attainment gaps need to be considered intelligently.

Figure 3 shows a fictitious example that depicts an ideal scenario in terms of data. It is important that schools ask themselves: is this a great place to learn if you come from a disadvantaged background? How do our disadvantaged pupils perform in relation to disadvantaged pupils nationally and locally? How do our disadvantaged learners fare compared with their more affluent peers?

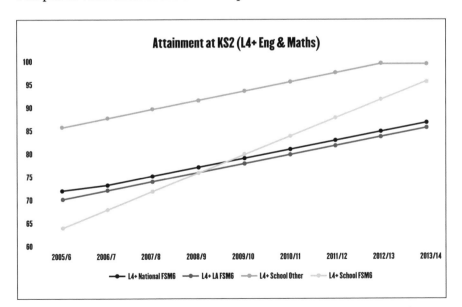

Figure 3: Raising attainment and narrowing the gap.

2. Complexities

One of the dilemmas many school leaders face is supporting vulnerable pupils who are not eligible for Pupil Premium funding. Juliette Jackson, a headteacher of three schools in Inner London, points out that some of the most vulnerable pupils in her care are those who come from 'minimum wage' families, where parent and carers work long hours, often in shifts, for little money. These families can be both materially poor and time poor. To tackle this problem, many schools have taken a pragmatic approach, providing resources and intervention at the point of need, and ensuring that the Pupil Premium funding is not diverted away from its target audience. Whilst schools are accountable for outcomes for disadvantaged learners, targeting the Pupil Premium on the classroom can have a positive impact on all learners within the 'Ever 6 FSM' category.

Within the 'Ever 6 FSM' category, the barriers to learning can be varied and complex. It is vitally important therefore to tailor Pupil Premium funded activity towards specific pupils, rather than just adopting a broad approach. Schools must set their own vision for their pupils, whether those with special educational needs (SEN), those who have English as an additional language (EAL), or those who are looked after children (LAC).

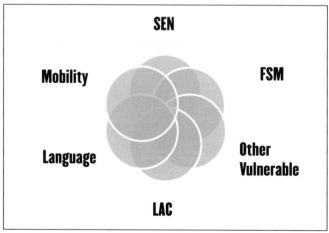

Figure 4: Some of the complexities for disadvantaged learners. Poverty may not be the primary factor preventing higher attainment.

One headteacher in the North East described a parent who arrived at her school with two children at his side. He announced that his children were coming to 'This school'. He did not know their names and the children had recently spent various periods in care. Catch-up classes with untrained teaching assistants are not going to overcome the challenges that children in these scenarios face. Such circumstances need high quality, tailored support and excellence in the classroom. At the same time we must avoid any sense of 'labelling' learners. The most effective schools have high expectation and high ambition for every pupil, regardless of background.

There are some other challenges to be wary of too – and these come with a word of warning that they are informed observations, and not from a statistical analysis:

- Many schools with high percentages of Pupil Premium students appear to do better as they have greater spending power, but context can affect this.

- Lower spending capability can mean a greater challenge for small schools and for those with low FSM numbers (for whom the increase in funding will be particularly welcome), though it can still be well spent on staff development and on partnerships with other schools.

- High Special Educational Needs (SEN) numbers within disadvantaged pupils can mean that low attainment is more difficult to shift; in some cases deprivation may not be the main determinate in lower attainment.

- This is also the case for many schools with high levels of children in care and for schools with high mobility. Counter-intuitively, it is not always the newly joined pupils who get stuck, as there is often a sharp focus on them as a vulnerable group.

To overcome these challenges, quality teaching and support staff across schools becomes even more important.

Roy Blatchford, Director of the National Education Trust, used to give a talk called 'Have you ever met a mugger who's read Middlemarch?' The key message is: whatever else we do in schools, think beyond accountability measures and make sure every learner leaves school with the dignity of being literate and numerate as a minimum. This will give young people some choice. At the same time, don't suppress your expectations of those from disadvantaged backgrounds. Seventeen Year 6 children from Grove Primary School in Handsworth, Birmingham secured a grade C in GCSE maths this year, nine of whom were eligible for the Pupil Premium. The school has over 60% of pupils from disadvantaged backgrounds, 77% of learners with English as an additional language, and has been securing good GCSE grades in mathematics for a decade.

'The Pupil Premium has enabled us to ensure that learning is more effectively transferred into life, improving the sustainable impact of the education we offer.'

Simon Knight, Special School Deputy Headteacher, Oxfordshire

3. Shallow Learning

The National Education Trust recently conducted a mathematics review for a school in the West Midlands. At first glance, the KS2 results look acceptable – nearly 90% L4+; a closer examination of the data showed that only a third of those children are L4b+. Children achieving a L4a have a 95% conversion rate to GCSE C+ in English and mathematics. With children at L4b or L4c that level is 72%. If the focus is solely on the accountability target of L4c, learning is not at the level it needs to be to ensure that children attain well and enhance their life chances. In this particular school, Pupil Premium funding is spent on 'one to one' in Year 6 and on teaching assistants.

One might think of this as the difference between organically farmed chickens, reared and nurtured as individuals, and battery hens – repeating the same task in the same place over and over again. The pressures are understandable, but to extend the metaphor just a little further, most of us prefer the idea of free range eggs over battery, even if it is harder work for the farmer, takes longer and is sometimes more expensive to achieve.

This 'shallow learning' approach is akin to filling up on confectionery to run a marathon. A child stumbling or being dragged to a Level 4c at the end of Key Stage 2 is like a refined sugar boost. It's briefly satisfying, but a few hours later there is an inevitable dip in performance.

Similarly, the L4c child, moving into a new learning environment and new learning culture, with outside influences increasingly impacting on their lives, can be lost in the challenging environs of the secondary school and its curriculum. Last minute booster classes to meet accountability measures create shallow learning. Sticking plaster solutions don't work – they fall off. Instead, schools must put into place well-researched, comprehensive, and flexible long-term plans if they want to address the fundamental barriers to learning and attainment.

4. Take Up

Many headteachers indicate that a number of pupils in their schools who are eligible for free school meals choose not to claim them, and thus the school does not receive its due funding. A common reason given for this is the social stigma attached to claiming free school meals; some schools find that after the introduction of a cashless system at lunchtime (hiding the identity of those claiming) the number of families applying for free school meals goes up.

One school offers families a 'learning voucher' worth £50 if they sign up for free school meals and another offers free uniform. This incentive is funded by the Premium itself. Another school offers a prize draw to encourage take up. Anyone who fills out a form, eligible or not, is entered to de-stigmatise application.

Non-take up of FSM is a challenge nationally (a DfE report says non-take up by eligible families stands at 11%[1]). Schools need to be proactive in encouraging take up: an increasing number of schools offer families a learning voucher to buy books, uniform or stationery for signing up, with some success. Universal Free School Meals (UFSM) means that primary schools need to be even more proactive in ensuring families 'sign up'.

Anecdotally, there is also a concern, especially because of the requirement to publish information about Pupil Premium funding on the school's website, that the Pupil Premium may create negative feelings between parents, with those *not* eligible feeling that their children are missing out unfairly. Headteachers have to walk a tightrope. It is crucial that school leaders ensure that all parents know and understand that the Pupil Premium can lead to whole school improvement. No one loses out if the whole class attains well.

5. The Department for Education (DfE) and the Pupil Premium

The consistent and important message from the DfE is encouraging, given some of the concerns school leaders have expressed. The DfE have emphasised that 'the government is quite serious in its ambition not to micromanage schools'; 'schools should be the decision-makers, using evidence to inform professional judgements'. The DfE has no particular view on using the Pupil Premium funding on whole-school initiatives (for example, teacher CPD on improving marking), as long as the attainment gap is closing, within a school context of generally improving attainment.

The DfE acknowledges the importance of pastoral initiatives to enable a child's readiness to learn, and point out that – in part – its national Summer School programme is based on this premise. Equally the Department warns against using the funding as a substitute for social welfare programmes which no longer exist. The clear message is that spending Pupil Premium on pastoral initiatives is fine as long as some thought has gone into how it will improve educational attainment, and how the impact will be measured.

The DfE takes a similar position on enrichment activities. It is important that enrichment activities have some educational goal if they are funded by the Pupil Premium (for example, improved science knowledge, or engagement in lessons). The DfE points out that schools still get a deprivation element in their mainstream dedicated schools grant (DSG), which can be used to subsidise trips that are not educational. Again, robust evaluation and clear success criteria are crucial.

Although the DfE has no pointed view on whole school approaches, if there were a situation where funding could either be spent on a non-FSM child who was underachieving, or an FSM child who was performing well, the funding should still be spent on the FSM child. It stresses that the Pupil Premium funding should not be conceptualised as a 'catch-up' initiative for underperforming students, and that attention and funding should be readily focused on those disadvantaged students who are performing well, to help them do even better.

6. Ofsted and the Pupil Premium

There is a concern that accountability measures might drive activity with the Pupil Premium and encourage the 'quick fix', or for schools to want to show they have spent the money on something physical, like iPads or a teaching assistant. However, Ofsted constantly reinforces the DfE's message that it is up to the school to decide how the Pupil Premium is spent, and confirm that there are no specific evaluation schedules or judgements to be made about Pupil Premium spending. Pupil Premium money can be spent 'where school leaders feel it is most needed'. However, the attainment gap and the impact of the spending are high profile issues for inspectors, and inspectors will want to see three key things:

1. A general trend towards closing the attainment gap within a context of generally improving attainment.

2. All pupils, including those eligible for the Pupil Premium, being tracked and making at least good progress.

3. Robust evaluation of any activity which is funded by the Pupil Premium.

Evaluation is not just about proving that something works. It is about understanding impact: Table 1.

Evaluation could include: the impact of short-term academic interventions on pupil attainment; the impact of longer term interventions, such as teacher training, on the quality of teaching or quality of feedback; or, for pastoral activities, parental questionnaires about attitudes to learning. A less robust approach, where schools simply state that 'we send pupils on trips to the theatre,' or 'we spend it on a nurture group led by a teaching assistant', is not good practice. Inspectors will want to hear what impact the theatre trip had, or what training the teaching assistant received, who was involved, what will the follow up be?

'The challenge for any school is to provide learning opportunities of the highest quality for all its pupils. The Pupil Premium has enabled us to create a place of excellence, endeavour and optimism.'

Sam Gaymond, Junior School Headteacher, Sheffield

Aim	Boost pupil progress through improved feedback	Evaluation
Actions	Cycle of CPD for staff	Monitor quality of CPD
	Additional time for staff for feedback	Monitor that additional time is being used effectively
Expected impact	Disadvantaged (target) Children to make XX months of accelerated progress	Baseline and post-trial discussions with staff and pupils

Table 1: Diagram of simple evaluation.

Ofsted recognises the concern raised by headteachers that there are vulnerable students in need of support who are not eligible for Pupil Premium funding, and give a pragmatic spending solution in response to this issue, which remains in line with the DfE's requirement to prioritise Pupil Premium spending on eligible students.

Put simply, if an intervention is required for 100 pupils and of these, only 60 are eligible for Pupil Premium funding, then 60% could be funded with Pupil Premium money (for accounting purposes), with the remaining 40% being funded by other sources. This allows schools to meet the needs of all the children in their schools, and use the Pupil Premium funding to create economies of scale. Ofsted have highlighted this approach in their most recent report on the Pupil Premium (*The Pupil Premium – how schools are spending the funding successfully to maximise achievement*, February 2013[2]).

When it comes to Ofsted and the Pupil Premium, leadership of the funding is again crucial. Headteachers need to be able to tell their school's Pupil Premium story when 'An Inspector Calls'. Schools do not want to be like the Birlings, finding it difficult to take responsibility, understand or articulate their role in the impact of the funding on pupil outcomes.

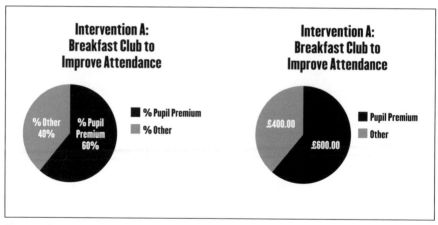

Figure 5: Ensuring Pupil Premium funds spent on disadvantaged learners.

Many schools are good at describing what they do with the Pupil Premium funding, but fewer can describe what impact it has. Regular tracking where the money is spent and what impact it is having is crucial from an Ofsted perspective, but it also allows for more effective use of the money, as interventions can be tweaked or changed if they are not having the intended impact.

Measurement of impact need not solely be based on attainment data, as for some interventions this may not be appropriate. It could be deduced from changes in attendance, progress in music, exclusion rates, pupil or parent feedback, observations or performance management and much more. At the same time, impact does need to be more than 'I enjoyed it...' Pupils have been known to 'enjoy' intervention because it gets them out of the classroom.

The most successful schools are thorough in their monitoring of every pupil, and thorough in their knowledge of every child. Good schools expect their Year 3 pupils to make the same progress over the year as their Year 6 pupils, so every member of staff feels equally responsible for the end of Key Stage results.

'Through the Pupil Premium our children have benefitted from real life experiences that have positively informed their academic and social learning journeys.'

Samera Ahmed, Primary Academy Vice Principal,
Reading

7. Parents

A key aspect of the Pupil Premium is effective communication with parents. Many colleagues ask about good examples of Pupil Premium statements on websites. It is important to keep things simple. Schools should ask themselves 'who is the message for?' and stick to the core facts: what are you spending the money on, why, and what impact are you expecting? Has it worked?

Rosendale Primary School in Lambeth provides an excellent example of this approach: *www.rosendale.cc/wp-content/uploads/2014/02/Pupil-Premium-Spending.pdf*.

Rosendale, like all successful schools, focusses its energies on the needs of their pupils and what happens *in the classroom* to improve outcomes for learners.

The school draws on research (no setting, no homework, offers time for teachers to provide quality feedback), understands the need to have the strong foundations for learning in place (attitudes, attendance, listening skills, language development, metacognition), and the blurring of the boundaries between the primary barriers to learning (SEN, deprivation *etc*).

Its Pupil Premium expenditure is underpinned by relentlessly high quality teaching, and the school teaches with open doors. For example, parents can attend lessons with their children once a week to improve parental involvement and attitudes to learning.

Hammond Academy, an excellent primary in Hemel Hempstead, uses a proportion of its Pupil Premium funding in vouchers for parents. Access to the grant is negotiated through highly skilled, highly committed Parent Partners who help broker appropriate uses of funds which help overcome barriers to learning. Underpinned by excellent teaching and very high expectations, the school focusses on the cultural gap and the engagement gap as a way of breaking down barriers to young people achieving their potential. More information about the school's use of the Pupil Premium can be found at: *www.hammondacademy.org.uk/88/pupil-premium*

8. Collaboration

Partnership working can be a significant weapon in narrowing the gap. The Pupil Premium resource can go even further through the use of economies of scale, especially for schools with fewer disadvantaged students. Genuine partnership like this is all too rare.

Estelle Morris famously challenged Oxfordshire Heads to 'give' their best teacher to the struggling school down the road in the spirit of partnership. That level of collaboration across the country may be some way off, but the notion of sharing is one to be embraced – with a careful understanding about how best to collaborate. As one headteacher observed wryly, 'if the children can share a mattress, we should be able to share a maths teacher.'

The National Education Trust has been working with a group of schools in a remote rural area. The group included three isolated primary schools from a series of linked villages. They didn't even share lifts to the CPD session – forget sharing a specialist maths teacher! They do both now, bursting with ambition to make things better. Courage to do things differently is needed by leaders, both headteachers and governors.

How can we ensure that under-performing schools look outwards, develop a culture of restlessness to improve, and are able to learn from others?

Genuine collaboration is a vitally important issue for education. The National Education Trust has produced a guide to effective partnerships entitled *Beyond Show and Tell*, which is available free from: *www.nationaleducationtrust.net/SchoolImprovementServices/beyondShowAndTell/ShowAndTellDownload.pdf*[3]

Without genuine and effective collaboration, the Pupil Premium policy will serve only to enhance gaps, because whilst good schools speed off into the distance, those falling behind will continue to look inwards, doing more of the same and trying to free themselves from regular inspection. If this happens, there is a risk that the Pupil Premium funding itself may be reduced, restricted or even stopped.

Nicola Shipman from the Steel City Partnership of Schools in

Sheffield tells a powerful story of school-to-school collaboration within their Multi Academy Trust. Working to a shared vision, three primary schools have undertaken a range of partnership initiatives to narrow gaps for disadvantaged learners. These include a move from 'continual professional development' to 'joint practice development', much of which is focussed on lesson study to improve the quality of teaching and team work. Every teacher across the partnership has an individual coaching plan. Action research takes place across the partnership on sharply focussed questions such as 'How are Teaching Assistants used?' or 'How has the teaching of history impacted on literacy across schools?'.

Pupil Premium children are tracked very closely, with regular professional conversations between teachers and leaders – so an understanding of successes and challenges are well understood by the directors of the Multi Academy Trust. The schools have adopted an immersive curriculum which is relevant to the needs of the Sheffield community the schools serve. The expectation that children must complete multiple drafts of work to ensure depth of knowledge and understanding before moving on to the next topic is vital for all learners.

The schools also use more straightforward techniques to try to improve outcomes. Free breakfast club if children attend on time for 10 days in a row has been quite a success! For further information visit: *http://steelcityschoolspartnership.info/SCSP/?page_id=120*.

9. Active Ingredients: Case Studies

The Education Endowment Foundation Guide offers some insights into the Pupil Premium in individual schools, highlighted in the Foreword, but the real challenge is scaling things up, and that's where we reach a barrier.

The most important element of any initiative is the quality of the person delivering it. Strong relationships between teacher and learner are fundamental. This is a graph which plots impact against cost for various interventions.

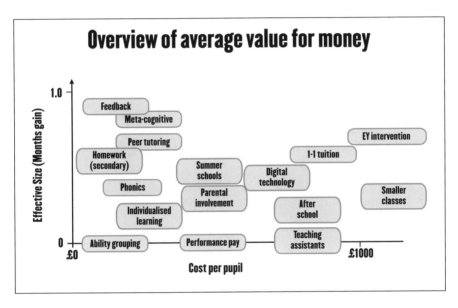

Figure 6: Overview of average value for money: Sutton Trust EEF – Teaching and Learning Toolkit.

This work by the Education Endowment Foundation has been transformational in encouraging schools to re-think their approach to narrowing gaps. But it is crucial that schools interrogate evidence and interpret what it might mean for their own institution.

The initial evidence of impact for Teaching Assistants (TAs) was controversial. It suggests that TAs are not the most effective way of raising attainment. However, there is a drive and passion in many teaching assistants to have a positive impact.

It is important to understand that, whilst the pay is low, full-time TAs are a £20,000 flexible resource which can be nurtured and grown, so we should *expect* an impact. We need to reflect on how to make sure that TAs realise their potential. Teaching assistants change lives at their best. To make this point, Charlie Henry HMI says that he rarely criticises teaching assistants, but he regularly has to criticise the management of them.

If we have professionally trained teaching assistants, working consistently, accessing model professional development and being well led and managed, then they will move across the arc on the EEF graph and become better value for money.

Recent evidence published by the EEF supports the view that high-quality, well-trained, and expertly deployed teaching assistants have a positive impact: *http://educationendowmentfoundation.org.uk/ news/teaching-assistants-can-improve-numeracy-and-literacy-when-used-effectively/*. Sometimes, it is not *what* you do but *how* you do it.

The National Education Trust has put together a checklist to think about in relation to effective use of Teaching Assistants:

- Are you giving regular appraisal to the TAs?
- Do you require minimum qualifications and/or experience?
- Do you ensure you provide reasonable and high quality CPD opportunities for support staff?
- Do you provide reasonable opportunities for joint planning?
- Do your support staff get high quality performance management?
- Do you have a system which formally requires TAs to record their impact on pupils' progress each week?

- Have you accessed good practice resources and case studies on TA deployment?

- Have you audited TAs' wider skills? (Many schools are missing out on hidden talents, especially in relation to languages, vocational skills and more.)

The EEF toolkit is very useful on many levels. Equally it is important to reiterate that schools must properly engage with current research and not follow it blindly without considering the context of their own school. Schools might say they have 'done' feedback or metacognition, but it is important to interrogate evidence carefully. Be *informed* by it and reflect. Pause... Research should not create unchallengeable orthodoxies or stifle innovation. An evidence-informed profession will develop from the classroom, where teachers learn from the toolkit. Teachers can ensure that their practice in its unique context is informed by evidence. A profession that effectively evaluates what it does is critically important.

The consistent feature of 'what works' for Pupil Premium pupils works for *all* pupils. Excellent teaching is crucial. The University of York publication *Effective Classroom Strategies for Closing the Gap in Educational Achievement for Children and Young People Living in Poverty, Including White, Working Class Boys*[4] explains this expertly. Feedback, at the top of the impact and value for money in the EEF toolkit, is about good teaching.

Charlie Henry HMI, Ofsted's lead for special educational needs, outlines the 'what works for some works for all' point when speaking powerfully about the ingredients of success for SEN pupils. They are:

- High aspirations for the achievement of pupils.

- Good teaching and learning for all pupils.

- Provision based on careful analysis of need, close monitoring of each individual's progress and a shared perception of desired outcomes.

- Evaluation of the effectiveness of provision at all levels in helping to improve opportunities and progress.

- Leaders who look to improve general provision to meet a wider range of needs rather than always increasing additional provision.

- Swift, timely changes to provision, by individual providers and local areas, as a result of evaluating achievement and well-being.

- Clear and detailed understanding of 'next steps', based on shared perceptions of the desired outcomes.

- Focus on pupils' starting points – exceeding expected progress.

- Regularly and accurately monitored data on the progress and attainment of pupils.

- Extensively evaluated interventions.

- Evaluating a wide range of data and using it effectively to improve standards and better provision.

There is nothing surprising on this list, and of course, many SEN pupils will also be eligible for Pupil Premium. This makes adopting best practice all the more important. However, not all schools act on, or feel able to act on, the available information.

The actions highlighted as being most cost-effective by the Education Endowment Foundation are not surprising either. But effective feedback, teaching children metacognition, and collaborative learning are all *hard* to do well, and to sustain. They are about consistently excellent teaching. Spending money on increasing leadership capacity and securing high quality professional development to ensure excellence is critical.

★★★★

There is a risk that teachers and school leaders see the Pupil Premium as encouragement for the idea that you can 'buy' something that is going to fix the complex range of challenges that are associated with poverty. Schools cannot prevent poverty, but they can go some way to reducing its effect if they focus on initiatives that raise attainment by improving teaching and learning, directly or indirectly. Teaching quality counts most.

To give an example, on a visit to a school during a recent Pupil Premium review, there was a breathtakingly good teaching assistant leading a reading recovery session. Seeing a little boy – starting the class with his shoulders slouched, looking down – coming to life and making visible progress in learning to read was incredibly moving. The key issue was that it was no way evident that the person leading the session was a teaching assistant. Impact counts.

This is where high quality professional development matters. Professor Robert Coe describes the kind of professional support which can best help learners. It should be:

- Intense: at least 15 contact hours, preferably 50.

- Sustained: over at least two terms.

- Content focused: on teachers' knowledge of subject content and how students learn it.

- Active: opportunities to try it out and discuss.

- Supported: external feedback and networks to improve and sustain.

- Evidence-based: promotes strategies supported by robust evaluation evidence.

Effective leaders recognise the importance of well constructed, in-house professional development, and ensure that their Pupil Premium funded activities are delivered by high quality, trained staff, with a clear understanding of the objectives of the programme. As a result, they invest in teacher and support staff training, which impacts on learning.

Case Studies – differing approaches to narrowing the gap

A. Lillington Primary School (Warwickshire) invested heavily in 'Outstanding Teacher Training Intervention' for five of its teachers as part of its wider strategy to improve pupil outcomes. The school measured impact carefully, spent time discussing strengths, weaknesses and areas for improvement (rather than getting bogged down in giving Ofsted-style grades), and ensured intervention was evidence-based and only delivered with excellence. Enrichment and pastoral activities run alongside teaching improvements. All pupils have a learning mentor so that every child is stretched as an individual, regardless of their starting point.

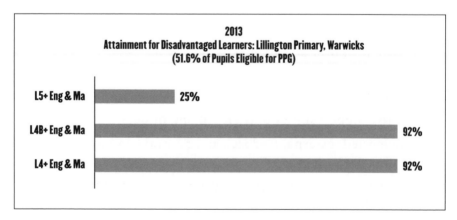

Figure 7: Attainment for Disadvantaged Learners at Lillington Primary School, Warwickshire.

'*The Pupil Premium has helped to turn the spotlight on the most vulnerable children in our country. It has challenged us not to think of short term alternatives to support these learners, but to fundamentally change their day to day experience of schools.*'

Steve Davies, Secondary School Headteacher, Sheffield

This school not only saw a dramatic improvement in its quality of teaching and SATs results, as well as a narrowing of the gap; it also saw a dramatic drop in teacher absence and its work with the Pupil Premium has been highly commended nationally.

The Head of Lillington Primary school recognised the need to focus on the team he worked with, to improve the teaching quality so that disadvantaged learners could catch up. He also recognised that there are no quick fixes. This has been transformational for learners. Further details at: *www.lillingtonschool.org.*

★★★★

B. Raynham Primary (Enfield) was struggling to improve their pupils' attainment levels. They tried intervention through teaching assistants and through graduates, but they were unsuccessful. There was limited impact despite extensive training. So they introduced a programme where retired, experienced teachers in their 70s, who no longer wanted to work full time, led the interventions. The scheme has been enormously successful. It's been jokingly called *Teach Last...* and it has had a sustained effect on pupils' outcomes.

These experienced teachers capitalise on their years in the classroom. Using detailed data analysis of individual children, they work with small groups to address 'shared gaps', assess pupil understanding and address needs so that pupils can quickly return to the classroom.

One of the aspects that stands out in much of the debate about improving outcomes for learners is a lack of reference to the curriculum. To promote deep rather than shallow learning, schools like Raynham link changes to the curriculum with their plans for the Pupil Premium. Schools which are successful in raising attainment for disadvantaged children have committed teachers, a whole-community ambition, a culturally relevant curriculum, and a vision for pupils which runs through the school as consistent as Brighton through a stick of rock. Further details at: *https://maps.google.com/maps/place?ie=UTF-8&q=raynham+primary+school+enfield&fb=*

★★★★

C. Bishop Challoner Catholic Girls' School (Tower Hamlets)
has demonstrated rapid success in supporting the progress and attainment of disadvantaged pupils.

As a school in a Local Authority identified as having the highest levels of child poverty in the UK, many students experience in some way the known effects of poverty and deprivation: low levels of aspiration and expectations; poor literacy and numeracy; lack of cultural enrichment; lack of family experience of university and professional careers; broken family structures; poor diet.

With over 50% of the school identified as disadvantaged under the Pupil Premium indicator, the senior leadership team made the acute analytical decision that funding should be used to impact on whole school improvement and transformation across the local federation.

The principle vision is that improving the quality of teaching and learning in all lessons and expanding the capacity of the federation means that all pupils benefit. The vision includes individualised, specific and methodical support over a period of time which has a clear focus on English, mathematics and science.

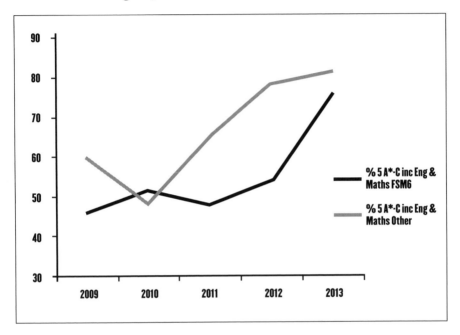

Figure 8: Attainment Gap at Bishop Challoner Girls' School 2009-2013.

Further details at: *https://plus.google.com/111352771309514080395/about?hl=en*

★★★★

D. Oakdene Primary (Stockton-on-Tees) is an excellent school in exceptionally challenging circumstances which declares that the sparkling curriculum, moulded and shaped to generate interest and intrigue in their pupils, their families and their teachers, is key to its success. This is backed up with the Pupil Premium being used to train and develop teachers and support staff to have the tools, expertise and knowledge to teach that curriculum so that children, often living difficult lives, are leaving with high attainment and a deep love of learning.

The rich community-relevant curriculum – a great mix of romance and rigour – means that the funding is used, indeed is targeted, to meet the needs of every learner in a school community with over 50% of learners from disadvantaged backgrounds, many of whom have special educational needs. Further details at: www.sbcschools.org.uk/oakdene.

★★★★

E. St Joseph's Catholic Primary (Camden) provides one of the most interesting examples on how to use the Pupil Premium. Its achievement statistics speak for themselves:

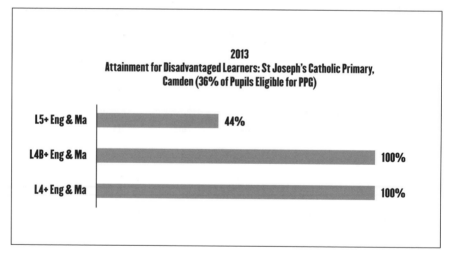

Figure 9: Attainment for Disadvantaged Learners at St Joseph's Catholic Primary School, Camden.

The inner urban school takes the view that – to offer children exceptional life chances – at the end of Key Stage 1, every child, regardless of background, should attain a Level 2b+. At the end of Key Stage 2, 100% of pupils should be at Level 4a+, 70% of pupils at a secure Level 5+ and 30% of children at Level 6 in maths.

The school's mantra is ambition, creativity and expertise, saying it is the responsibility of the school to enable the child to make progress, clearly demonstrating that equal opportunity is not the same as equal provision.

Spending money on	Impact/Benefit /Enables
Increase capacity of SLT: *The Leadership taking responsibility*	To run and monitor interventions across the school To ensure T&L are good or outstanding To provide effective training for ALL staff To work with outside agencies and vulnerable children
EY Intervention	To identify vulnerable children who need additional support and plan provision To provide parent workshops in literacy and maths
Extracurricular trips and activities	To enhance the curriculum, ensure children are able to participate, and to give children the opportunity to experience new and challenging activities
High quality and focussed training for all staff – including specialist subject knowledge	To ensure that children have personalised support to meet their needs So highly trained TAs run evidence based interventions To develop and grow a specialist maths teacher
Increase capacity to run catch up programmes	To accelerate progress in maths and literacy in KS2 to ensure children are working at or above age related expectations
Funding club activities	To ensure the children are able to participate and to give children the opportunity to experience new and challenging activities outside of school
Achievement for All	Achievement for All is a whole-school approach to school improvement, which has had demonstrable success in improving rates of progress for vulnerable pupils.

Figure 10: Pupil Premium Statement: St Joseph's Catholic Primary School, Camden 2013/14.

Put simply, the school leadership takes ownership. They create the time, space and capacity to ensure excellence as standard in everything they do. Further details at: *www.stjosephs.camden.sch.uk/ PDF%20Policies/Premium.pdf*

★★★★

10. Special Schools

Special Schools need to evaluate the degree to which socio-economic background is impacting on outcomes. In doing this, they need to consider to what extent the socio-economic background is either a greater limiting factor than the learning disability, or the extent to which it provides a different challenge from that posed by the learning disability.

In Special School provision there are interesting questions about how the additional funding can be utilised in such a way that it will have a meaningful impact on pupil outcomes. This is because the primary barrier to learning is usually developmental rather than socio-economic.

When planning for the use of the Pupil Premium, **Frank Wise Special School** in Oxfordshire looked beyond the notion of successful outcomes being based on knowledge and skills and also considered the application of what has already been learned within functional contexts.

This enabled the school to identify where socio-economic background may begin to influence more, particularly around the further development of socially appropriate behaviours and socially based communication.

The difficulty is that access to effectively staffed, developmentally and age-appropriate social opportunities can be limited, expensive and logistically challenging. Yet without access to such experiences there is a risk that children may not be able to apply the social and communication skills being developed at school.

To overcome this challenge in a sustainable way, the school used Pupil Premium funding to contribute to the employment of an Out of School Liaison Officer (OSLO) to secure further funding for access and act as a broker between providers of social opportunity and families who may want to take up those opportunities but have practical barriers to overcome.

The OSLO is an integral position in the school, supporting the school's aim and ethos. This helps to promote the school's philosophy within the local area, developing a community-wide belief in the potential of school pupils, recognising they have both the right and ability to be active contributors to the community in which they live.

★★★★

The Pupil Premium Plus is potentially a great boost for special schools, for many will get an increase in funding as pupils with SEN are disproportionately 'looked after'.

Limpsfield Grange School is a special school in Surrey for girls between the ages of 11-16. The school also offers residential provision, which is accessed by the majority of students attending Limpsfield Grange across a school week. It caters for students with a wide range of needs including Autism and Asperger's; students who have communication and interaction difficulties; and students who due to their physical or emotional vulnerabilities would not have the resilience to succeed in a mainstream setting.

The spending offers a really interesting example of a school that has focused on ensuring that individual students in receipt of the

> *'We have high expectations for all of our pupils and the Pupil Premium Grant has supported us in providing personalised learning programmes to raise attainment and enrich the experiences of our more vulnerable pupils.'*
>
> Rosie Alexander, Primary Headteacher, Hertfordshire

Pupil Premium meet their bespoke targets. In particular the school has concentrated on developing literacy and numeracy skills for Pupil Premium learners in order to increase access to the rest of the curriculum.

The school uses a number of interventions to support improving literacy and numeracy skills including:

- GCSE Statistics for more able learners.
- Up-levelling writing groups.
- Spelling City.
- Mathletics for KS3 students.
- Comprehension sessions.
- Reading for meaning and developing inference skill sessions.
- GCSE booster sessions for English.

Many students have difficulties with their communication and interaction skills associated with their autism, mental health needs or due to the high levels of social anxiety that they experience. The majority of students at Limpsfield Grange also require high levels of support to help them to understand their own thoughts and feelings, and how these impact on other people. To support these needs, the school has used some of its funding for a Family Partnership Practitioner who has been working with identified students and their families to help promote communication and interaction skills, with the aim of enabling students to be able to identify and label their emotions. This improves the students' ability to be ready to learn, and enables them to access learning. This work has included:

- 'Drawing and talking' therapy sessions for small groups of identified students to develop self-awareness and identify strategies to help promote positive communication and interaction skills.

- One-to-one support with students with fixed and inflexible thinking to develop strategies for communicating with their peers.

- Running focus groups in the residential setting which work with identified students on their statemented needs.

- 'Sand Play' therapy sessions for students who have difficulty labelling and identifying their emotions.

- Supporting students access a self-esteem and body image course.

- How to stay safe on the internet sessions with students at risk of online sexual exploitation.

The school expects that these interventions will enable the identified students to improve their communication skills, their access to the curriculum and their engagement and attitude to learning. The senior leadership team monitor the pupil spend per pupil each week, and monitor outcomes and impact regularly to ensure that Pupil Premium money spent is directly linked to improved student outcomes. Interestingly, the school invites parents to speak with the leadership team if they have any concerns about how the funding is being used, linking back to the original mission to focus on the *individual*.

11. Looked After Children (LAC)

Children in care and children who have been adopted or who are on special guardianship orders or residence orders receive the Pupil Premium Plus, which is £1900 per annum. This funding is paid to schools for adopted and SGO/RO children, but the funding for children in care now goes to local authorities for the head of the Virtual School to manage. This postholder – a statutory requirement for local authorities under the Children and Families Act 2014 – carries out the duty of local authorities to promote the education of children in care.

Children in care are amongst the lowest performing groups of any children. In 2013, only 15.3% attained five or more GCSEs at A*-C including English and mathematics, and only around 30% made three or more levels of progress from Key Stage 2 in English or mathematics. Only 58% of 19 year-old care leavers were in education, employment or training in March 2013.

The gaps at Key Stages 1 and 2, though narrower, are still concerning. Children in care are ten times more likely to have a statement of SEN than their peers (severe SEN can mean that parents and carers struggle to cope), and are more likely to be excluded. Frequent changes of carers and schools usually compound the problem. There is less evidence about the attainment of adopted/SGO/RO children but the message is clear – children who have endured early abuse and neglect can hugely underachieve in education, even if they have lived in caring and supportive homes for many years.

So, what works? All of the strategies listed in the Education Endowment Fund toolkit are just as applicable to children in care. Small group tuition, though expensive, is regarded by many to be one of the most effective strategies since a good tutor will identify the gaps in learning and teach accordingly.

Evidence to support this comes from several sources including the Department for Education and research by Robert Flynn[5] in Canada. The Department for Education also identifies the following as crucial to educational success:

- Placement stability – of home and school.
- Length of time in care – the longer a child is in one care placement the better they are likely to achieve.
- Attending a school that meets the child's assessed needs, *ie* high academic expectations.

However, often the missing ingredient is a shared professional understanding and language between schools, social workers and carers of the effects of trauma on a child's capacity to succeed within school. Attachment and trauma have long been a part of social care and carer training but for some reason it has largely bypassed teacher training and school-based professional development.

Recent neuro-scientific research now underpins earlier psychological research and shows how the affected child's brain simply isn't wired to cope with schooling. If you've grown up in fear, unable to control your anger or impulses and believe you are worthless then schools, however welcoming, seem like hostile battlegrounds; lessons – intriguing and challenging to most – can trigger overwhelming stress[6].

We still have distance to travel before arriving at a school system better attuned to help these most vulnerable children cope, but work by writers like Louise Bomber[7] point the way. What is also needed is hard edged research to show what works for the children when nothing else in the teacher's toolkit seems to.

12. Transition

Transition from primary to secondary school is a critical time for disadvantaged learners. When resilience and focus in learning are needed most, the tectonic plates of school culture and environment shift markedly under the feet of children who are making the leap at 11+.

The failure to improve the process of transition is one of the major challenges facing our education system. It is a problem that seems often to be ignored by policy makers, and the accountability chasm encourages inertia in tackling the problem system-wide. However, there are effective actions which schools can take tomorrow:

1. To encourage sharing in the use of the Pupil Premium in the long term, primary schools often keep a file with a record of interventions which FSM children have taken part in, and their impact. This can be passed on to secondary schools so that they can target their resources more appropriately.

2. Children should take books with them into Key Stage 3 to enable teachers to get a deeper understanding of strengths and weaknesses in primary school. Key Stage 3 practitioners should also have a good understanding of the Primary National Curriculum.

3. Create a Year 7 playground to ease children into secondary school life.

Transition means that less resilient learners are at risk of falling further behind during what can be a daunting experience. Special schools and those schools with high numbers of service families children are rich resources for effective approaches to transition. When systems work well, these schools prepare for the individual pupil, making sure that children arriving at their new school glide into the new learning environment, rather than land with a crash. The principle is that the destination school and class needs to be prepared for the arriving

'When used well, Pupil Premium
has the possibility to open up a
whole new world for a child who
may never have experienced what
you and I may have always taken
for granted.'

Vanessa Langley, Executive Headteacher, Sheffield

learner, as well as the child being prepared for their new school.

Clearly there are challenges to recreate such highly personalised approaches at scale, but at the same time it is important to learn from what can work. The Education Endowment Foundation has a growing bank of national research on successful approaches to transition, but it is local leadership and collaboration which are crucial.

Most importantly, we must avoid at all costs a culture of dismissing prior learning in Key Stage 2 at secondary level. At the same time, the shallow learning approach, as described in chapter three, where children are pulled up through repeated SATs practice to meet accountability targets in Year 6, only serves to enhance the view of some Key Stage 3 teachers that many children cannot successfully access the secondary curriculum. A better grasp of a learner's strengths and weaknesses can help negate these views, as can a better understanding of progress up to and during transition.

Barriers to learning that are common in disadvantaged pupils, with a change of schools, and curriculum, exacerbate the challenges for less resilient learners.

Teaching metacognition may well be the key. Research at Rosendale Primary School in Lambeth indicates that metacognition can help create successful learners who have:

- Clear understanding of what they do and do not know.

- Ability to plan an approach to problems.

- Ability to seek out information.

- Ability to check on their progress.

- Ability to change strategies when things go wrong.

These characteristics may sustain learners during the period of transition. By teaching children metacognition in Year 6, with those themes picked up again in Year 7 to ensure a continuum, learners can go back to what has helped them previously to overcome future challenges.

Whatever actions schools take, the fog of accountability targets and responsibility for outcomes should not deter schools from ensuring that all learners have solid foundations, and that the building blocks are secure to enable learning continuity during one of the most vulnerable times in their schooling.

13. Governance

Governors have a crucial role to play in ensuring that Pupil Premium activity has the maximum impact and value for money. Informed discussions with governors from good schools demonstrate an understanding of activity and impact of the Pupil Premium in their school. Governors and leaders also need to have discussions about what to *stop doing* because it is not working so well.

Nationally, governance is patchy with the Pupil Premium, but a leading example is a Special School we have worked with in the Midlands. Governors there have a detailed knowledge of the range of activities undertaken with Pupil Premium funding, as well as an understanding of the aims and actual impact.

There is a clear channel for regular updates on activity and impact. Governors receive details of pupils (anonymised) in receipt of Pupil Premium funding. They are informed about what individual pupil requirements are, what intervention each pupil receives, what impact is expected and a summary evaluation for each pupil.

> *'A personalised curriculum is fundamental to meeting the individual learning needs of our pupils. Pupil Premium is key in helping us to achieve this.'*
>
> Derek Fance, Primary School Headteacher, Warwickshire

Information is also provided at a higher level, with governors informed about the effect of particular interventions on groups of pupils, as well as the overall impact of a range of interventions on an individual pupil. This allows governors to act as 'critical friends' to the school, and ensure that the Pupil Premium is being spent in a way that has most benefit; it enables a professional discourse.

Our work nationally on governance shows that challenge and support are of varying quality. There are some excellent examples of good practice, but also a significant minority of governors who have very limited knowledge of the attainment gap in their school, how much money is received, how it is being spent and what the impact of funding is.

In effective governing bodies, the three keys are:

- Training is given for governors on evaluating the impact of interventions on attitudes, learning behaviours, well-being, aspirations and other outcomes as well as on academic measures.

- Governing bodies nominate an interested and committed Pupil Premium governor to work with the school leadership team to ensure there is secure knowledge across all governors of Pupil Premium funded activity and impact.

- Most governors can answer the questions in the analysis and challenge for schools (see page 69).

14. Successful Schools and the Pupil Premium

In his remarkable book *The Diving Bell and the Butterfly*, Jean Dominique Bauby narrates his story by blinking one eyelid whilst experiencing 'locked-in syndrome'. The metaphor is that his body is weighed down by the diving bell of disability, whilst his mind is still free to 'write' what has been described by the *Financial Times* as 'one of the great books of the century'.

Bauby offers two thoughts which one might relate to disadvantaged learners. First, the Pupil Premium cannot entirely negate the effects of poverty on learner outcomes, but it is part of the package which schools can use to set children and young people free from the diving bell of the circumstances into which they are born. Second, it is a reminder that limits should not be set on what learners can achieve, in spite of or because of their circumstances.

Schools which are successful with raising expectations and outcomes for Pupil Premium children share key common characteristics:

- Firstly, quality of teaching and learning counts most. Schools that create the best outcomes for pupils, recruit, train and retain great teachers and support staff. They adhere to model practice in the use of professional development. If the teaching is not consistently very good at your school, then that should be the focus for Pupil Premium funded activity – any other initiative is sticking plaster.

- Secondly, understanding attitudes to learning and family engagement, on a pupil-by-pupil basis, is vital for the successful impact of Pupil Premium spending. This is a big challenge, and one identified as 'the next step' for many school leaders, however successful they have been in narrowing gaps.

- Thirdly, successful schools build teams where their vision is understood and pursued by the entire school community with relentless energy. Visit Slough and Eton CE Business & Enterprise College, St Mary's CE Primary in Handsworth, The Wroxham School in Hertfordshire, Frank Wise Special School in Banbury, St Eugene De Menezes Catholic Primary in Camden, or Oakdene Primary in Stockton and ask any member of teaching staff about the school's vision. The vision runs consistently through the school, imprinted in its DNA. Aspirations are values driven.

One of the consistent features of excellent leaders is that they understand their communities to the point that they know what it is like to live their lives. As Harper Lee writes in *To Kill a Mockingbird*: 'You never really understand a person until you consider things from his point of view – until you climb into his skin and walk around in it.'

It is in these schools that we see national and local trends robustly challenged, with disadvantaged pupils performing at the levels their peers do nationally. These primary, special and secondary schools:

- Are open to sharing what they do, at the same time constantly looking outwards, to learn from others and to 'magpie' ideas.

- Work together to make transition almost seamless.

- Plan for the long term, asking: 'what will work in our school context, excite pupils and their families about learning'? It's not just the Pupil Premium that will help narrow the gaps.

- Have high expectations and take risks to reach their goals – they don't let accountability targets drive practice. As Phillip Pullman writes in his memorable children's horror story *Clockwork*: 'You don't win ... by wishing. You have to train hard, strive your upmost and sometimes that isn't enough. You have to be willing to risk failure.'

- Use data to inform their practice and interventions, but don't let it become their Sargasso Sea – not everything can be measured in the same way and it is important not to get bogged down. Learning how to evaluate effectively is crucial.

15. Top Tips

Over the past three years across the country – with an appreciative focus on the impact of the Pupil Premium – the National Education Trust has held seminars, conferences and meetings with headteachers, additionally conducting many interviews with pupils and observing significant numbers of classrooms. As an independent foundation we applaud this government initiative, and salute the many ways in which teachers and school leaders are making a real difference to children's and young people's lives through creative, innovative and often exemplary use of the allocated funding.

Reflecting sharply on all that we have seen, we present the following Top Tips. This is not a definitive list and we invite readers to add their own recommendations, and share them with us via *marc@ nationaleducationtrust.net* – for future editions of this Guide.

- Use the BAR approach: Identify **Barriers** > Agree **Actions** > Evaluate **Robustly**. Be clear about expected impact, monitor quality.

- Stop or change course if things are not working.

- Know what the attainment gap is, how much Pupil Premium funding the school receives, how your school is spending the money, what the impact is, and how you are evaluating for 'next steps'.

- Harness your funding to support and stretch higher attainers. Eligibility does not mean low attainment.

- Don't pigeon-hole disadvantaged children as low attainers who are culturally illiterate and disinterested. Ava Sturridge Packer of St Mary's CE Primary School in Birmingham speaks powerfully about children from disadvantaged backgrounds and minority ethnic groups going to the ballet. Enable all children to experience those things perhaps associated with middle-class families.

- Linger over language. The language gap is one of the biggest causes of underachievement in later life, especially for disadvantaged learners.

- Step back from your school – look up, look out at what other colleagues are doing. Just like a great painting, you'll see your school more clearly from a distance.

- Challenge orthodoxies: children at Level 4c in Year 6 can go to Year 4 for peer tutoring, which improves attainment for younger children and embeds knowledge for older children, with no stigma about 'going back'.

- Go Pupil Premium 'speed dating' with a group of local schools. Hear what people are doing, chose something that interests you, and go and see it.

- Be wary of expensive conferences on Pupil Premium. There are no shortcuts!

- Resist the temptation to be 'busy' with your funding. If you need to spend your funding on retaining a great teacher, or creating capacity in your leadership team to support, coach and monitor, then spend it there. If you need to improve subject knowledge in Years 3 and 4, so the last two years are not spent catching up, spend it there. Focus on long-term, sustained impact.

- Trust staff, and make them feel trusted. Provide time and space for well-designed research projects which will have a positive impact on pupil outcomes. If the research shows no effect, don't continue down that route. This will create a culture of openness and continuous learning.

- Use the 'Test and Learn' approach for introducing new Pupil Premium funded activities. Supermarkets when introducing a new product will not stack the shelves of every shop in the country. They will introduce carefully – check impact, tweak and change. Once perfected, the product will be rolled out.

- With intervention, look for low effort, high impact. Ask 'can the intervention be sustained?' Louize Allen of the Lambeth Teaching Schools' Alliance talks about the 'Gaudi Test' for interventions and initiatives – will someone value it enough to continue and complete it once you've moved on?

- Self-evaluate regularly. Ask your senior leadership team to write a short report on what Ofsted would say about your school's use of the Pupil Premium. Review this once a term.

- Beware of averages as an outcome. Setting a target of 'average attendance of 95%' for disadvantaged students may mask poor attendance for some children who have very complex barriers to learning. Set your target high for *every* pupil.

- Focus on progress to improve *attainment*. A student cannot put on their CV that they got a grade D in GCSE maths but that they made excellent progress.

- Use funding to enable inexperienced teachers, or those who are struggling, to observe excellent practice. Then coach them for improvement.

- Conduct a skills and subject knowledge audit. Include teaching assistants in this process.

- Create time for your team. We have yet to meet a teacher or leader who doesn't value space to read, research or reflect.

- Remember children have hidden talents outside of the classroom. Encourage them to be developed, nurture the privilege of childhood and it might spark something amazing!

Overcoming the achievement gap is challenging. There are no quick fixes. Closing the gap requires risk taking and taking people out of comfort zones, but in a system where currently just a third of poorer pupils make the grade, we cannot afford to do nothing.

The Pupil Premium might just be the key that unlocks the opportunity for *everyone* to attain well.

> *'Pupil Premium Plus for children in care can transform lives that have hitherto seemed without hope. Bespoke support for learning helps them grow stronger than the neglect and abuse that put many of them in care in the first place.'*
>
> Mike Gorman, Headteacher, Virtual School for Looked After Children, Bath and North East Somerset

16. Sample Pupil Premium Reviews

A. New End Primary School

	L4+ Reading, writing and maths	L4b+ Reading, writing and maths	L5+ Reading, writing and maths
Disadvantaged	100%	89%	29%
Other	88%	67%	23%
Gap	-12%	-22%	-6%

FSM6	36%	SEN	4%
FSM	27%	EAL	12%
NOR	367	Absence	4.8%

New End Primary is an average sized primary school. The percentage of disadvantaged children is slightly higher than the national average. The percentage of children who have special educational needs and those who speak English as an additional language is relatively low.

The school performs very well in respect of the percentage of disadvantaged children reaching expected attainment levels at the end of Key Stage Two, with 100% of learners achieving Level 4+ and 29% learners achieving Level 5+ in reading, writing and maths. Disadvantaged learners outperformed their peers in 2013.

The School's approach to improving outcomes for disadvantaged learners dovetails with the school's overarching mission:

- Enable every child to fulfil their potential, with a personalised education that meets the needs of each pupil.

- Help every pupil develop the skills, knowledge and personal qualities needed for life.

This mission is underpinned with an approach that states on the school's website that 'All pupils are taught according to their needs and ability whether they are eligible for the Pupil Premium or have other barriers to learning'.

The primary aim is to offer consistently high quality teaching that will help learners overcome any barriers they face to attain well. The school also works to tackle underlying issues such as negative attitudes to learning and the associated problems this brings. Inspectors have commented on the excellent attitudes to learning that are consistently visible across the school.

The need for a consistency of approach and the understanding of the school's mission are evident throughout the school, in classrooms and in the wider learning environment – but it can be particularly evidenced through the spending of Pupil Premium, which is used to:

- Employ well-qualified teachers and teaching assistants.
- Purchase resources and equipment for children with additional needs.
- Train staff on how equipment can be used to achieve the best results.
- Provide rewards and merits to encourage children to achieve, and also to improve pupils' attitudes including punctuality and improvements in attendance.

The Pupil Premium enables learners to be taught (when necessary) in small groups or individually in order to improve their attainment and progress. Specifically (part) funded by Pupil Premium are:

- High quality, well qualified support staff who are assigned to a particular class providing intervention (for example, evidence-based programmes such as Numicon) where necessary, and working with teachers to ensure differentiation that enables all children to make at least good progress.

- An SEN Support Teaching Assistant who works across the school supporting individuals both in and out of the classrooms, making sure that they all make the necessary progress throughout their time at the school: 'No child left behind.'

The school's focus on excellence in their support staff, who are clear about their roles and the expectations of them, is striking. Support staff receive high quality professional development that is sharply focussed on the needs of children.

The school makes clear in its Pupil Premium statement that not all children who are eligible for the Pupil Premium receive direct intervention funded by the grant. Rather, intervention is directed where it is needed, with all pupils eligible benefiting from the focus on the quality of teaching, the quality of resources and the training staff receive to make the best of those resources. This is evidenced by the fact that higher attainers from disadvantaged backgrounds are performing well.

The school has engaged in some very interesting work to develop socially engaged learners who understand the world around them. This work includes building respect and understanding for the environment and its resources. Using outside expertise to engage learners of all abilities, children benefit from building their language, developing their speaking and listening skills, their understanding of history and their environment, as well as improving their ability to work as a team, a fundamentally important life skill.

The leadership of the Pupil Premium at New End Primary is excellent. The headteacher and assistant headteacher (who has been moved to a non-class-based role to monitor, support and coach for high quality in the classroom) take considered responsibility for the quality of the school's work to create resilient, successful learners, regardless of their background.

★★★★

B. Heath Down Primary School

2013 KS2 SATS	L4+ Reading, writing & maths	L4b+ Reading, writing & maths	L5+ Reading, writing & maths
Disadvantaged	41%	42%	0%
Other	90%	83%	21%
Gap	49%	41%	21%

FSM6	22.1%	SEN	6.5%
FSM	18.4%	EAL	14.2%
NOR	576	Absence	4.9%

Heath Down Primary is a large school. The majority of pupils are of white British heritage. The proportion of pupils that speak English as an additional language is relatively low, though this figure is increasing. The proportion of pupils known to be eligible for the Pupil Premium is low, though numbers are still significant in a large school. The percentage of pupils with special educational needs is low.

Whilst attainment across the school is slightly above the national and LA average, there is a significant gap between the attainment levels of disadvantaged children and their peers in 2013. No children from disadvantaged backgrounds reached Level 5+ in reading, writing and maths, compared to 21% of 'other' children.

The SENCO at the school has a good knowledge and understanding of the effective use of the Pupil Premium. Detailed tracking information and provision maps for children eligible for the Pupil Premium are in place, but there is a disconnect between the information flowing between the classroom and what is being held centrally. More effective systems for **information sharing** could ensure that the needs of individual learners are understood and shared between those involved in the management, class teaching and intervention. A shared approach for teachers and support staff to help identify key issues and challenges would also help better planning for children's needs.

Pupil Premium funded activities such as one to one tuition are delivered by high quality, committed staff, and the children taking part make some progress in their sessions. However, this does not always translate into improved progress and attainment outcomes, suggesting that the intervention work needs to be more effectively dovetailed with the wave one teaching and other support / intervention. Greater clarity about proposed outcomes for interventions would help the school distil what impact activities are having, as opposed to them broadly aiming to improve overall progress and attainment.

The school's self evaluation statement and school action plan recognise the strengths and weaknesses of the school in respect of the Pupil Premium, but needs to go further in explaining intended outcomes from funded activity, and how impact will be evaluated. The quality of delivery, implementation and CPD are of greater importance than the type of activity undertaken.

Next steps:

- Improve the general understanding about effective practice in using the Pupil Premium across *all* school staff.

- Through staff meetings, document sharing and systems that ensure all staff:

  a. understand aims and high expectations for individual Pupil Premium children.

  b. understand their role in raising attainment for these children.

- Randomly select six children as a case study to see what effect information sharing has had on children's progress and attainment. Obtain feedback from child, teacher, TA and those leading any interventions before, during and after the project takes place.*

- Visit a school, in a similar context, which is performing well with its disadvantaged learners.

Robust evaluation is crucial here. Poorly designed evaluation means you will not be able to tell whether any initiative has worked or not, and so whether it is worth continuing. Poorly designed evaluation leads to poorly understood results.

★★★★

Note: For further information about commissioning **Pupil Premium Reviews,** led by the National Education Trust, please contact marc@nationaleducationtrust.net

★★★★

DfE Performance Tables for Featured Schools

St Joseph's Catholic Primary School, Camden
www.education.gov.uk/cgi-bin/schools/performance/school.pl?urn=100041

Raynham Primary School, Enfield
www.education.gov.uk/cgi-bin/schools/performance/school.pl?urn=102023

Hammond Primary Academy, Hertfordshire
www.education.gov.uk/cgi-bin/schools/performance/school.pl?urn=137238

Rosendale Primary School, Lambeth
www.education.gov.uk/cgi-bin/schools/performance/school.pl?urn=131335

Oakdene Primary School, Stockton on Tees
www.education.gov.uk/cgi-bin/schools/performance/school.pl?urn=131409

Bishop Challoner Catholic Girls School, Tower Hamlets
www.education.gov.uk/cgi-bin/schools/performance/school.pl?urn=100978

Lillington Primary and Nursery School, Warwickshire
www.education.gov.uk/cgi-bin/schools/performance/school.pl?urn=130869

About the National Education Trust

The National Education Trust (NET) was created in 2006 as an independent charitable foundation. We harness our extensive national and international experience to bring about improvements for learners, from early years to university entrance. We assist education leaders and practitioners in sustaining success and tackling underperformance. Our knowledge and expertise enable us to lead and support policy reform, rooted in what works in the classroom.

An on-going priority for the Trust is closing 'the achievement gap', a stubborn feature of our education system. Working with schools, the third sector, local and national government, and other education agencies, we are at the forefront of initiatives to improve educational outcomes for all.

The Trust has three key platforms:
1. A National Resource for high quality practice in teaching and learning
2. An independent provider of high quality professional development
3. An intelligent contributor to education policy, debate and reform.

www.nationaleducationtrust.net

★★★★

With thanks to:
Lucy Crehan
Mike Gorman
Simon Knight
Stephen Rodwell
Hammond Academy, Hemel Hempstead
Frank Wise Special School, Banbury
Lillington Primary School, Leamington Spa
Oakdale Primary School, Stockton on Tees
Raynham Primary School, Edmonton
Rosendale Primary School, Lambeth

St. Joseph's Catholic Primary School, Camden
Bishop Challoner Girls School, Tower Hamlets
Bath and North East Somerset Virtual School for Looked After
Children
Limpsfield Grange Special School, Surrey

★★★★

References

1 Anthony Lord, Jenny Easby and Helen Evans, DfE (2013) *Pupils
not claiming Free School Meal – 2013: Research Report.*

2 Ofsted (2013) *The Pupil Premium: how schools are spending the
funding successfully to maximise achievement.*

3 Professor Derek Bell (2013) *Beyond Show and Tell.* Available at
www.nationaleducationtrust.net/SchoolImprovementServices/
beyondShowAndTell/ShowAndTellDownload.pdf

4 Centre for Excellence and Outcomes in Children and Young
People's Services (2011*): Effective classroom strategies for closing the
gap in educational achievement for children and young people living in
poverty, including white working-class boys.*

5 Flynn, R. see special issue of Children and Youth Services
Review, 34 (6), June, 2012, on improving educational outcomes of
young people in care.

6 Cozolino, L. (2013) *The Social Neuroscience of Education.*
W. W. Norton & Company: New York, London.

7 Bomber, L. (2011) *What About Me? Inclusive Strategies to support
pupils with attachment difficulties make it through the school day.*
Worth Publishing.

Part Two

Ofsted guidance – analysis and challenge tools for schools

The following information accompanies Ofsted's Pupil Premium report (January 2013). It contains a series of tools that schools can use to help them to analyse where there are gaps in achievements between pupils who are eligible for the Pupil Premium and those who are not, and to plan the action they need to take.

Age group: 5–16
Published: January 2013
Reference no: 130045

Contents

Analysis and challenge toolkit for school leaders: secondary

On the following pages are modified versions of the tables used by inspectors during the Pupil Premium survey. Schools could use these to inform discussions between school leaders and governors, and help to shape future strategic planning for the use of the Pupil Premium funding. The tools could also be used to aid self-evaluation and may help with preparing for a section 5 or section 8 inspection. The tables can be adapted for future use by changing the dates. They could also be adapted to focus on achievement gaps for any other groups in the school.

Data for the pupil outcomes table for Year 11 should be taken from RAISEonline.
Data for other year groups should be available from the school's own tracking of pupils' attainment and progress.

Financial year	Amount of Pupil Premium funding
2011-12	
2012-13	
2013-14	

	2011-12		2012-13
Percentage of FSM pupils			
Number of FSM pupils eligible for the Pupil Premium	@£488	=	@£623
Number of looked after pupils eligible for the Pupil Premium	@£488	=	@£623
Number of service children eligible for the Pupil Premium	@£200	=	@£250
Total			

Where are the gaps in Year 11?

Year 11: Indicator (using data from RAISEonline for 2011 and 2012, and school data for current Year 11. Definition of FSM for this purpose is the same as RAISE – those pupils eligible for the Pupil Premium under the 'Ever 6' measure. LAC and service children in later section).	2011 gap between FSM and non FSM	2012 gap between FSM and non FSM	2013 predicted outcome for FSM	2013 predicted outcome for non FSM	2013 predicted gap	Comments/ contextual information
Attainment – 5+ A*-C passes including English and mathematics						
Attainment – average points score in English						
Attainment – average points score in mathematics						
Attainment – average points score (best eight GCSEs)						
Attainment – average points score (best eight GCSEs including equivalents)						
Achievement – expected progress in English						
Achievement – more than expected progress in English						
Achievement – expected progress in mathematics						
Achievement – more than expected progress in mathematics						
Achievement – value-added score (best eight GCSEs)						
Achievement – value-added score (best eight GCSEs including equivalents)						
Attendance						
Persistent absence						
Fixed-term exclusions						

Where are the gaps (other year groups)?

Year group	What does your data analysis tell you about the relative attainment and achievement of FSM and non-FSM pupils for each year group? Are there any gaps? To what extent are gaps closing compared with previous years' data?
Year 7	
Year 8	
Year 9	
Year 10	

Where are the gaps (other eligible groups)?

Group	Comment on predicted outcomes in 2013 and any gaps. Consider attainment, progress, attendance and exclusions.
Looked after children	
Service children	

Reflective questions

To what extent are the strengths and priorities suggested by this data clearly evident in the school's self-evaluation and improvement plans? If any are missing, outline them below and add them to your improvement plan, or use the separate planning and evaluation outline on page 12.
Which strengths are not reflected in your self-evaluation?
Which priorities are not reflected in your school improvement plans?

Analysis and challenge toolkit for school leaders: primary

On the following pages are modified versions of the tables used by inspectors during the Pupil Premium survey. Schools could use these to inform discussions between school leaders and governors, and help to shape future strategic planning for the use of the Pupil Premium funding. The tools could also be used to aid self-evaluation and may help with preparing for a section 5 or section 8 inspection. The tables can be adapted for future use by changing the dates. They could also be adapted to focus on achievement gaps for any other groups in the school.

Data for the pupil outcomes table for Year 6 should be taken from RAISEonline.

Data for other year groups should be available from the school's own tracking of pupils' attainment and progress.

Financial year	Amount of Pupil Premium funding
2011-12	
2012-13	
2013-14	

	2013-14		2014-15	
Percentage of FSM pupils				
Number of FSM pupils eligible for the Pupil Premium	@£	=	@£	=
Number of looked after pupils eligible for the Pupil Premium	@£	=	@£	=
Number of service children eligible for the Pupil Premium	@£	=	@£	=
Total				

Where are the gaps (Year 6)?

Year 6: Indicator (using data from RAISEonline for 2011 and 2012, and school data for current Year 6. Definition of FSM for this purpose is the same as RAISE – those pupils eligible for the Pupil Premium under the 'Ever6' measure. LAC and service children in later section).	2013 gap between FSM and non FSM	2013 gap between FSM and non FSM	2014 predicted outcome for FSM	2014 predicted outcome for non FSM	2014 predicted gap	Comments/ contextual information
Attainment – Level 4+ in English						
Attainment – Level 4+ in mathematics						
Average points score – English						
Average points score – reading						
Average points score – writing						
Average points score – mathematics						
Achievement – expected progress in English						
Achievement – more than expected progress in English						
Achievement – expected progress in mathematics						
Achievement – more than expected progress in mathematics						

Attendance						
Persistent absence						
Fixed-term exclusions						

Where are the gaps (other year groups)?

Year group	What does your data analysis tell you about the relative attainment and achievement of FSM and non-FSM pupils for each year group? Are there any gaps? Is there evidence of closing gaps compared with previous years' data?
Early Years Foundation Stage	
Year 1 (consider whether pupils are making expected progress on the basis of their Early Years Foundation Stage score; consider the phonics screening check)	
Year 2 (consider predicted end of Key Stage results for reading, writing and mathematics at each sub-level, as well as current data)	
Year 3	
Year 4	
Year 5	

Where are the gaps (other eligible groups)?

Group	Comment on predicted outcomes in 2013 and any gaps. Consider attainment, progress, attendance and exclusions.
Looked after children	
Service children	

Reflective questions

To what extent are the strengths and priorities suggested by this data clearly evident in the school's self-evaluation and improvement plans? If any are missing, outline them below and add them to your improvement plan or use the separate planning and evaluation outline on page 12.
Which strengths are not reflected in your self-evaluation?
Which priorities are not reflected in your school improvement plans?

Planning and evaluation outline

Pupil Premium used for:	Amount allocated to the intervention / action (£)	Is this a new or continued activity/cost centre?	Brief summary of the intervention or action, including details of year groups and pupils involved, and the timescale	Specific intended outcomes: how will this intervention or action improve achievement for pupils eligible for the Pupil Premium? What will it achieve if successful?	How will this activity be monitored, when and by whom? How will success be evidenced?	Actual impact: What did the action or activity actually achieve? Be specific: 'As a result of this action...' If you plan to repeat this activity, what would you change to improve it next time?

Self-review questions for governing bodies

Governors' knowledge and awareness

1. Have leaders and governors considered research and reports about what works to inform their decisions about how to spend the Pupil Premium?
2. Do governors know how much money is allocated to the school for the Pupil Premium? Is this identified in the school's budget planning?
3. Is there a clearly understood and shared rationale for how this money is spent and what it should achieve? Is this communicated to all stakeholders including parents?
4. Do governors know how the school spends this money? What improvements has the allocation brought about? How is this measured and reported to governors and parents via the

school's website (a new requirement)?
5. If this funding is combined with other resources, can governors isolate and check on the impact of the funding and ascertain the difference it is making?
6. Do governors know whether leaders and managers are checking that the actions are working and are of suitable quality?

Leaders and managers' actions
1. Do the school's improvement/action plans identify whether there are any issues in the performance of pupils who are eligible for the Pupil Premium?
2. Do the actions noted for improving outcomes for Pupil Premium pupils:
   - give details of how the resources are to be allocated?
   - give an overview of the actions to be taken?
   - give a summary of the expected outcomes?
   - identify ways of monitoring the effectiveness of these actions as they are ongoing and note who will be responsible for ensuring that this information is passed to governors?
   - explain what will be evaluated at the end of the action and what measures of success will be applied?
3. Is the leader responsible for this area of the school's work identified?
4. How do governors keep an ongoing check on these actions and ask pertinent questions about progress ahead of any summary evaluations?
5. Are the progress and outcomes of eligible pupils identified and analysed by the school's tracking systems? Is this information reported to governors in a way that enables them to see clearly whether the gap in the performance of eligible pupils and other pupils is closing?

Pupils' progress and attainment
1. Does the summary report of RAISEonline show that there are any gaps in performance between pupils who are eligible for free school meals and those who are not at the end of key stages? (Look at the tables on the previous pages of this docu-

ment for some indicators to consider)

2. Do the school's systems enable governors to have a clear picture of the progress and attainment of pupils who are eligible for the Pupil Premium in all year groups across the school, not just those at the end of key stages?

3. If there are gaps in the attainment of pupils who are eligible for the Pupil Premium and those who are not, are eligible pupils making accelerated progress – are they progressing faster than the expected rate – in order to allow the gaps to close? Even if all pupils make expected progress this will not necessarily make up for previous underperformance.

4. Is the school tracking the attendance, punctuality and behaviour (particularly exclusions) of this group and taking action to address any differences?

Overall, will governors know and be able to intervene quickly if outcomes are not improving in the way that they want them to?

Reader's Notes

Reader's Notes

Reader's Notes

85

The Restless School

By Roy Blatchford

What do successful schools and their leaders have in common? They are restless. There is a paradox at their core: they are very secure in their systems, values and successes, yet simultaneously seeking to change and improve. These schools look inwards to secure wise development; they look outwards to seize innovation which they can hew to their own ends and, importantly, make a difference to the children and students they serve. That is the restless school.

"In this thought-provoking book Roy Blatchford draws on 40 years of wide ranging experience within the UK and international education systems in order to capture the essence of successful schools."

Brian Lightman, Association of School and College Leaders

"Blatchford sets teachers, schools and their leaders a standard that's terrifying in prospect, yet assuredly attainable if we can just maintain our courage, commitment and determination – our professionalism, indeed, as he stresses. Inspired by this remarkable small handbook of school excellence, I don't see how we can avoid accepting and confronting the challenge. It would be rude not to!"

Bernard Trafford, Headmaster, Royal Grammar School, Newcastle

"I wish I had read The Restless School in the early days of my teaching – indeed at any stage of my teaching. In a short and pacy book I found distilled everything that matters, all expressed in a generous, open and wise way. And it puts a spring in your step."

Jonathan Smith, author of The Learning Game

Roy Blatchford is Director of the National Education Trust. Previously he was Her Majesty's Inspector of Schools in England, with national responsibilities for school improvement and for the inspection of outstanding schools.

He is the author/editor of over 150 books and is a regular contributor to the national media. Recent books include Sparkling Classrooms, The 2012 Teachers Standards and Taking Forward the Primary Curriculum.

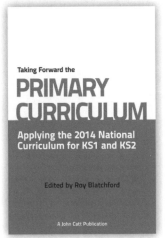

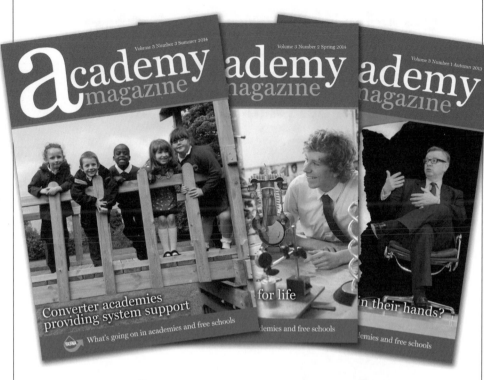

Academy Magazine

Launched in October 2011, Academy celebrates and supports the exciting, fast-growing academy and free school sectors in the UK. Written and read by all those with a professional interest in these state-funded independent schools, the magazine is partnered with FASNA (Freedom and Autonomy for Schools – National Association) and has quickly been recognised as an authoritative voice in the field.

Two-year subscriptions @ £25.00